Read, Learn & Create

THE OCEAN CRAFT BOOK

Clare Beaton
& Rudi Haig

illustrated by
Clare Beaton

iˑiˑi Charlesbridge

Oceans

mackerel

stingray

Oceans are huge bodies of salt water that cover almost three-quarters of Earth's surface. There are five oceans: the Arctic, Atlantic, Indian, Pacific, and Southern. There are also smaller seas, such as the Mediterranean and the Caribbean.

The billions of plants and animals that live in the ocean are different from those that live in freshwater, such as rivers or ponds. Oceans are very deep, and it's only in recent years that scientists have been able to explore the dark depths where even more creatures live.

Despite the huge size of the oceans, they are all under threat from pollution created by people. Oil spills, poisons from factories, and garbage in the water are killing seabirds, animals, and plant life. The danger is so great that people are making new laws to try to reduce the amount of plastic we use.

You can help, too, by never leaving litter on the beach and collecting garbage you find and disposing of it properly.

carrageen (Irish moss)

cuvie (forest kelp)

Penguins

Penguins are birds that cannot fly. They are usually found in colder climates, and they have flippers instead of wings, which make them very strong swimmers. In fact, they spend half their life swimming in water, where they catch and feed on fish and squid. There are several penguin species, each with a unique appearance. For example, the rockhopper penguin has yellow feathered eyebrows. All penguins have a black back and a white belly. Their coloring works as camouflage, making it more difficult to see them when they swim and protecting them from predators such as leopard seals.

African penguin

rockhopper penguin

baby emperor penguins

king penguin

Activities

Each topic in this book comes with a simple craft activity (and one has a yummy recipe!) for you to make at home. Here are some helpful hints to get you started.

Important! Remember to always get help from an adult before starting any project in this book.

Materials

It's useful to have some materials, such as empty cereal and tissue boxes, heavy paper, and paper-towel or toilet-paper tubes, ready for when you feel creative.

   Several activities in this book use recycled items, and perhaps you can think of more items to reuse.

How to Use the Templates in This Book

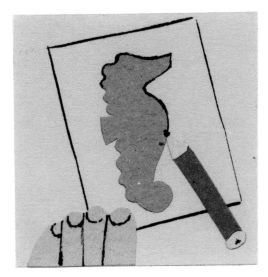

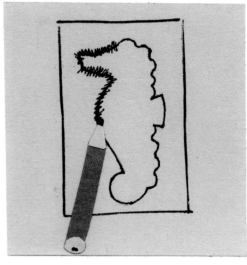

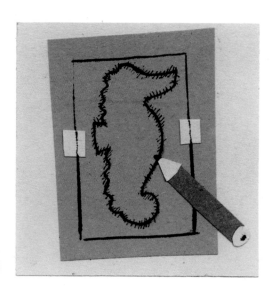

1 Place a piece of tracing paper over the template. Hold the paper steady and trace around the shape.

2 Turn your tracing paper over and gently scribble over the lines with a soft pencil.

3 Turn your tracing paper over again and tape it onto your craft paper. Retrace firmly over the original lines to transfer the shape.

TIP: You can use parchment paper instead of tracing paper.

Paper Cup Penguins

What You Will Need

plastic or paper cups (clean out used ones), black and white paint and paintbrushes, tracing paper, pencil, tape, black and yellow construction paper, scissors, black felt-tip pen, glue

1 Paint your cup(s) black, leaving a U shape on one side for the belly (see illustrations). If the cup is white, you can leave the belly part unpainted. If not, paint it white.

2 While the cups dry, decide which size templates go best with the size of your cup.

3 Trace the wing template twice onto black paper (see instructions on page 3).

4 Trace the eye template twice and the beak template once onto yellow paper. (Trace two eyebrow templates on yellow paper to make a rockhopper penguin.)

5 Cut out all your pieces.

6 Draw a black dot on the eye pieces and glue them in place on the cup. If you're adding eyebrows, cut short slits in the eyebrow piece (see illustration) and glue them on.

7 Ask an adult to use scissors to poke a hole in the cup where the beak will go. Wrap the beak piece to form a cone with a point and secure it with tape. From inside the cup, poke the beak through the hole, point first. It should stay in place without tape.

8 Glue the wings onto the sides of the cup with the tips pointing backward (see illustrations).

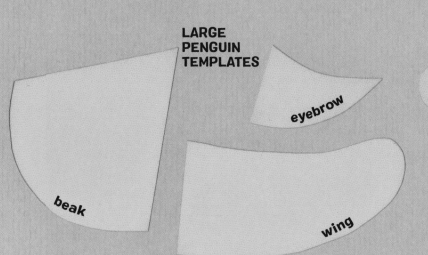

LARGE PENGUIN TEMPLATES

eyebrow

eye

beak

wing

loggerhead

TIP: If you use plastic cups, mix a tiny bit of liquid soap into the paint to help i

Sea Turtles

Sea turtles, also called marine turtles, are reptiles found in every ocean except at the polar regions, which are too cold for them. They are much larger than other turtles. They have a hard shell that acts as armor to protect them from predators. The top side of the shell is called a carapace.

There are seven different species of sea turtle, each with a different-shaped shell. The biggest is the leatherback, which averages six feet (2 meters) long and more than one thousand pounds (450 kilos). That's about the same size as a horse. Sea turtles cannot breathe underwater, but many can hold their breath for more than thirty minutes.

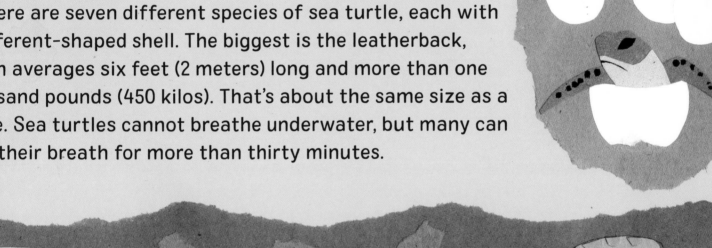

turtle eggs and a baby turtle hatching

turtle

leatherback turtle

green turtle

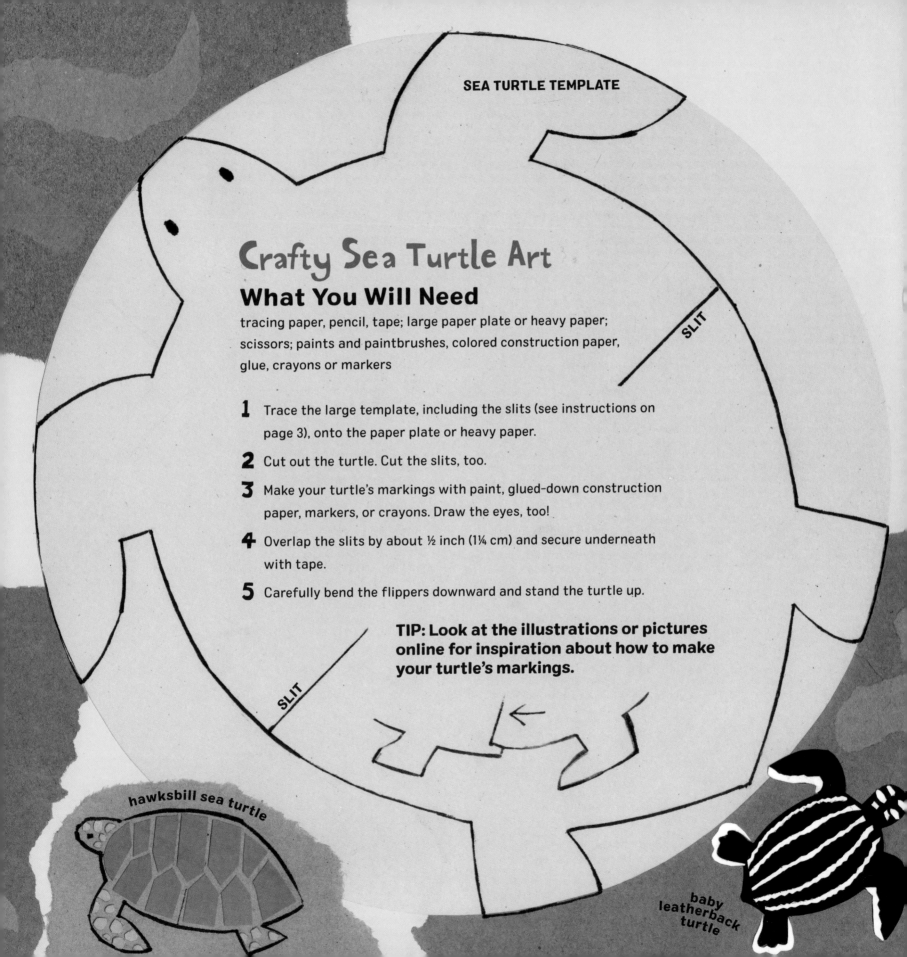

SLIT

Crafty Sea Turtle Art

What You Will Need

tracing paper, pencil, tape; large paper plate or heavy paper;
scissors; paints and paintbrushes, colored construction paper,
glue, crayons or markers

1 Trace the large template, including the slits (see instructions on
page 3), onto the paper plate or heavy paper.

2 Cut out the turtle. Cut the slits, too.

3 Make your turtle's markings with paint, glued-down construction
paper, markers, or crayons. Draw the eyes, too!

4 Overlap the slits by about ½ inch (1¼ cm) and secure underneath
with tape.

5 Carefully bend the flippers downward and stand the turtle up.

**TIP: Look at the illustrations or pictures
online for inspiration about how to make
your turtle's markings.**

SLIT

hawksbill sea turtle

baby
leatherback
turtle

Dolphins and Porpoises

bottlenose dolphin

common dolphin

Dolphins and porpoises are large marine mammals that are mostly found in shallow seas. Both are known for being very smart. Both use sonar, or sound, to move around safely underwater.

    Dolphins are usually gray and have longer noses and bigger mouths than porpoises. They also have a curved dorsal fin in the middle of their back and have leaner bodies than porpoises. Porpoises are often darker than dolphins, with a white or gray belly. They have small pointed flippers and triangular-shaped dorsal fins. Dolphins are more talkative than porpoises—they make sounds to communicate and navigate underwater.

harbor porpoise

Porpoise or Dolphin Wheel

What You Will Need

large paper plate (about 8 inches (20 cm) across); thick white paper; scissors; tracing paper, pencil, tape; markers, crayons, or paint and paintbrushes; blue construction paper; paper fastener

1 Trace the plate on thick white paper and cut the circle out.

2 Trace the dolphin or porpoise templates (see instructions on page 3) onto your white circle so they look like they are swimming in the same direction, as shown in the illustration.

3 Color or paint the dolphins or porpoises. (Give it time to dry!)

4 Cut the blue paper into a rectangle 12 inches (30cm) long and 8 inches (20cm) high. Cut waves along the top edge (see illustration).

5 Poke a small hole in the center of your white circle and one in the top middle of the blue rectangle. Line them up with the blue rectangle on top and secure with paper fastener. Fold the ends of the fastener flat.

6 Now turn the wheel to make it look as if the dolphins or porpoises are playing in the ocean.

DOLPHIN TEMPLATE

PORPOISE TEMPLATE

TIP: You could also make a whale or flying-fish wheel.

Sharks

bull shark

hammerhead shark

Sharks have existed for a very long time, appearing more than four hundred million years ago (before dinosaurs!). They usually live in salt water and have fins, gills, and snouts. There are about five hundred species of shark, and they vary greatly in size, shape, color, and behavior. The biggest is the gentle whale shark, which can be as big as a school bus. The smallest is the dwarf lantern shark, which is only about eight inches (20 cm) long! Great white sharks are the most famous shark. They are impressive hunters and can jump up to ten feet (3 meters) out of the water to catch their prey.

leopard shark

great white shark

blue shark

Shark Pop-Up Card

What You Will Need

white 8½ x 11 (letter size) paper, ruler, pencil, markers, scissors

1. Fold the paper in half and in half again.

2. Open one fold. Measure 3½ inches (9 cm) from the top and draw a line 2½ inches (6½ cm) long. (See illustration.)

3. Draw a zigzag line through the line you just drew—this is your shark's mouth. Using the illustration as a guide, draw the outline of the frontal view of a shark and the eyes.

4. Color in the shark, leaving its teeth white.

5. Open the paper and cut a slit along the horizontal line. (See illustration).

6. Place your finger into the slit and gently pull up while also closing the card, folding the mouth into a triangle. Close and press it down. (See illustration.) Do this again, pulling down for the bottom of the mouth.

7. Fold your card in half and write whatever you wish on the front. When your friend opens the card—the shark bites!

TIP: You might want to practice making the mouth on some scrap paper first before making your card.

basking shark

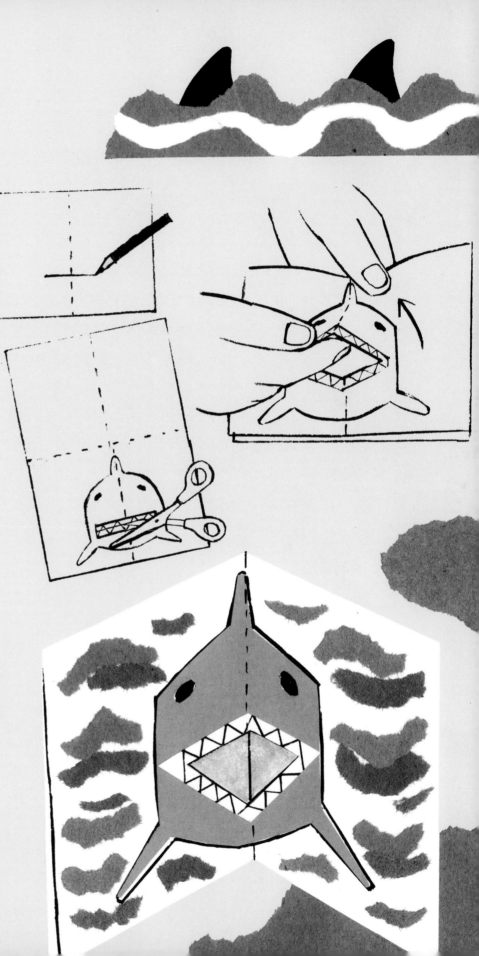

Unusual Fish

catfish

hairy frogfish

Some creatures in the ocean have a strange or funny appearance, especially those that look like animals or objects found on land. In fact, there are many fish that are named after the animals they resemble (look at the illustrations on this page for examples). The longhorn cowfish is a type of boxfish with horns that stick out of the front of its head, like a cow's. The hairy frogfish is a carnivore—a meat eater—that looks similar to a frog and moves like one, too. Their fins act like legs, and they use them to move slowly over the seabed, where they lie in wait for their prey.

mousefish

clownfish

parrotfish

longhorn cowfish

Colorful Fish Creations

Make one of the fish illustrated here or think up your own!

What You Will Need

tracing paper, pencil, tape; thick paper; scissors; markers; decorations such as sequins, glitter, and stickers; glue; yarn and/or popsicle stick

1 Trace the fish template onto the thick paper (see instructions on page 3) and cut out.

2 Decorate the fish however you like on both sides.

3 Poke a small hole at the top of the body and attach a length of yarn to hang the fish, or tape the bottom of the fish onto a popsicle stick and use it like a puppet.

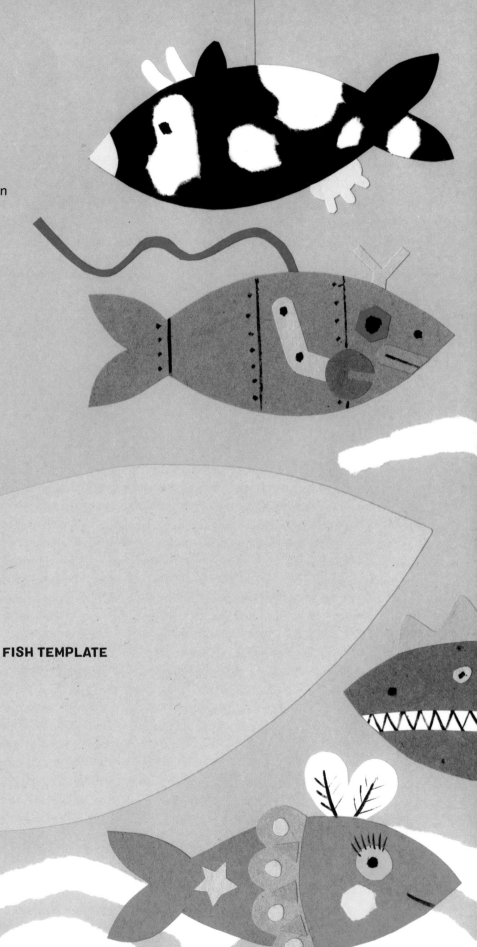

FISH TEMPLATE

Luminous Creatures

Antarctic krill

Commerson's frogfish

anglerfish

bluebottle

luminous brittle star

deep sea worm

There are some parts of the ocean that are very deep. The deepest part is 36,000 feet (11,000 meters)—that's about how high planes fly in the sky. It is very dark because sunlight can't reach so deep. Many sea creatures that live very deep produce their own light. It is called bioluminescence. Creatures glow and glitter for many reasons. Anglerfish dangle a lighted lure in front of their mouth to attract prey. Deep-sea worms produce different lights to communicate with one another. Bioluminescence can also protect animals by scaring or confusing predators.

Ocean Boats

motorboat

sailboat

fishing boat

The only way for people to travel long distances across seas and oceans is by airplane or boat. Sailboats use sails—structures made of special fabric—to capture the wind and move across the water. Much bigger boats such as ferries and cruise ships use engines for power.

Some boats have jobs to do, such as lifeboats that rescue passengers of other boats from dangerous situations or bad weather. Tugboats push or pull larger vessels that have mechanical issues or are too big to navigate busy harbors or narrow canals by themselves.

motor lifeboat

tugboat

Recycling Crafts

Next time you walk on a beach, take a bag or pail with you to collect things you find. You could find smooth driftwood, plastic pieces, nylon rope, shells with holes in them, and more. Be sure to leave anything sharp or still alive behind.

What You Will Need

whatever you find on the beach, plus optional items depending on what you'll make, such as string, glue, paper clips, cardboard box

1 Rinse everything you find in cold water and leave it to dry.

2 What you find will help you decide what to make. Be creative!

3 Use string, glue, or paper clips to attach items to other items.

4 To make a display, divide a cardboard box into sections, arrange your collection, and make small signs to mark where you found each item.

5 See the illustrations for more ideas.

TIP: Have fun making something from found items and feel good about helping to clean up the beach!

Beachcombing

Visiting the beach when the tide is out to search for interesting or valuable items is called beachcombing. You can also help keep the beach clean by picking up plastic and other trash. You can recycle what you find on the beach or use it to make crafts.

A beach is never the same from one day to the next. Almost anything could wash up. You might find shells, crab shells, sea glass, and broken bits of pottery. Maybe you'll even find a lump of rare and valuable ambergris—a smelly wax-like substance made by sperm whales and used to make perfume.

Your Own Coral Reef

What You Will Need:

paper-towel and toilet-paper tubes, small cardboard box or box lid, paints and paintbrushes, pencil, construction paper, scissors, markers, sequins, glitter, glue and/or tape

1 Paint the tube corals whatever colors you like. Paint the box or lid a different color—this will be your base. Leave everything to dry.

2 Cut some coral shapes out of construction paper (see illustrations). Decorate both sides with paint or markers. Let them dry.

3 Draw and cut out fish from construction paper. (Maybe use the fish template on page 13 or the seahorse template from page 17.) Decorate both sides.

4 Stand the box or lid so the closed side is on top. Arrange the tube coral standing up on the surface and draw around each with a pencil. Cut holes slightly inside the lines you drew (so the tubes will fit firmly). Cut slits for your shapes. Then carefully push the tube corals into the holes and the coral shapes into the slits.

5 Glue or tape the fish onto the coral reef. Glue on glitter or sequins if you like. (See the illustration for ideas.)

TIP: You could add shells, octopuses, and other creatures to your reef.

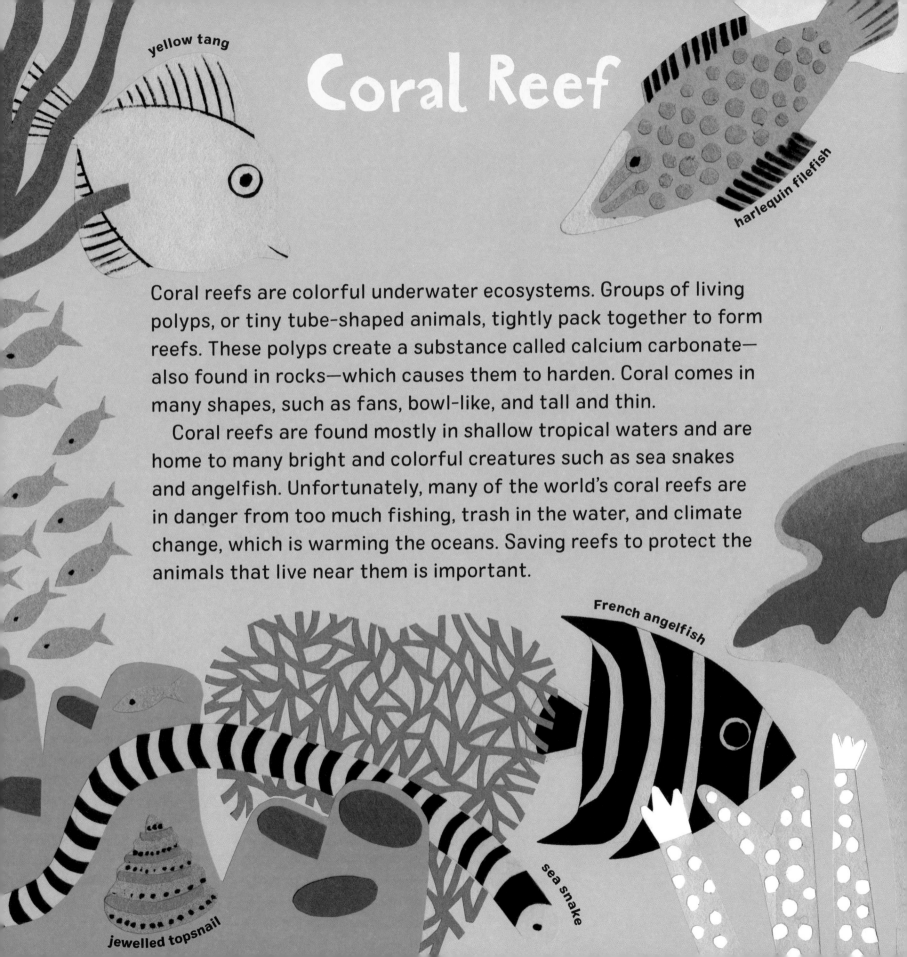

Coral Reef

yellow tang

harlequin filefish

Coral reefs are colorful underwater ecosystems. Groups of living polyps, or tiny tube-shaped animals, tightly pack together to form reefs. These polyps create a substance called calcium carbonate—also found in rocks—which causes them to harden. Coral comes in many shapes, such as fans, bowl-like, and tall and thin.

Coral reefs are found mostly in shallow tropical waters and are home to many bright and colorful creatures such as sea snakes and angelfish. Unfortunately, many of the world's coral reefs are in danger from too much fishing, trash in the water, and climate change, which is warming the oceans. Saving reefs to protect the animals that live near them is important.

French angelfish

jewelled topsnail

sea snake

Toilet-Paper Tube Crab

What You Will Need:

toilet-paper tube, scissors, masking tape, orange paint and paintbrush, two black buttons, glue, black felt-tip pen

1 Cut the tube into three pieces, one bigger than the other two (as shown in figure 1).

2 Cut one of the smaller rings and unroll it into a strip. Cut claws on the ends (as shown in figure 2).

3 Cut the other smaller ring and unroll it into a strip. Cut off 1 inch (2½ cm) and discard. Then cut the ends into four points for the legs (as shown in figure 3).

4 Slightly squash the larger ring by pressing down on it gently. Push the claw strip through so there is a claw on each side (as shown in figure 4), then tape the strip inside the ring to secure it.

5 Push the leg strip through so one leg is on each end (as shown in figure 4) and tape to secure it.

6 Paint your crab orange and leave it to dry.

7 Glue on the buttons for eyes and draw a mouth.

hermit crab

1

2

3

4

limpet

Ocean Floor

great scallop

common mussel

The ocean floor is home to lots of sea life, including more than five thousand species of crab. Some crabs, such as the giant Japanese spider crab, are as wide as a car. Others, like the pea crab, are as small as . . . a pea! All crabs have a shell body with two pincers, or claws, and four pairs of legs that they use to move sideways.

Not all animals on the ocean floor have bones or shells. Anemones are colorful jelly-like creatures that look like they have lots of fingers. They can climb onto objects and stick, and they are venomous, which means they can make other animals sick by stinging them.

common lobster

common winkle

common gray sea slug

anemone

Jellyfish Bowl Bouncer (or Hat)

What You Will Need

colored thin plastic (reuse plastic shopping bags!); scissors;
white paper bowl; tape; yarn, string, or elastic cord; colored paper;
glue; markers

1 Cut the plastic into thin strips of different lengths and shapes.

2 Tape one end of each strip into the inside of the bowl. Make sure
to tape strips all around the bowl.

3 Poke a hole in the center of the bowl and push the yarn, string,
or elastic cord through, knotting the end to keep it in place.

4 Decorate the bowl by gluing on colored paper or drawing on it
with markers.

5 Hold the end of the string and bounce the jellyfish as if it
were swimming.

**TIP: You can make
a jellyfish hat by
attaching the string to
each side of the bowl to
make a strap.**

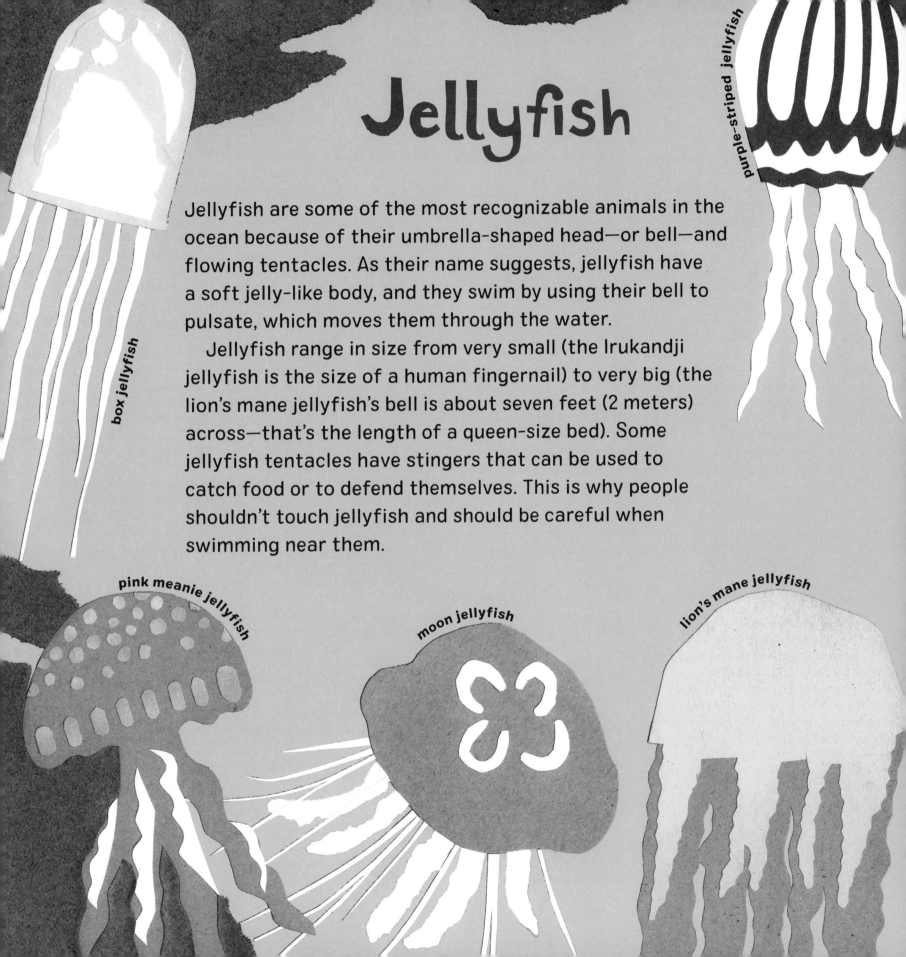

Jellyfish

Jellyfish are some of the most recognizable animals in the ocean because of their umbrella-shaped head—or bell—and flowing tentacles. As their name suggests, jellyfish have a soft jelly-like body, and they swim by using their bell to pulsate, which moves them through the water.

Jellyfish range in size from very small (the Irukandji jellyfish is the size of a human fingernail) to very big (the lion's mane jellyfish's bell is about seven feet (2 meters) across—that's the length of a queen-size bed). Some jellyfish tentacles have stingers that can be used to catch food or to defend themselves. This is why people shouldn't touch jellyfish and should be careful when swimming near them.

purple-striped jellyfish

box jellyfish

pink meanie jellyfish

moon jellyfish

lion's mane jellyfish

Starfish Cookies
What You Will Need

1 cup all-purpose flour (and extra for surfaces), 1½ teaspoons baking powder, ½ teaspoon salt, ⅝ cup of room-temperature butter (and extra for greasing pans), ½ cup granulated sugar, 1 egg, beaten

1 Mix the flour, baking powder, and salt in a large bowl. Fork in the butter until it forms fine crumbs.

2 Add the sugar and the egg and mix into a stiff dough. Knead the dough on a lightly floured surface until smooth. Form into a ball.

3 Cover the dough in foil or plastic wrap and chill in the fridge for 30 minutes.

4 Preheat the oven to 350°F. Grease cookie sheets with butter.

5 Roll out the dough about ¼-inch (½ cm) thick on a lightly floured surface and cut out stars with a cookie cutter. Using a spatula, place the cookies on cookie sheets and prick lightly with a fork.

6 Bake for about 12 minutes, or until the cookies are golden brown. Wait two minutes and transfer to a cooling rack.

Icing
What You Will Need

1 cup powdered sugar, 2 tablespoons boiling water, yellow or orange food coloring

1 Put the sugar in a bowl and gradually add the hot water while mixing to a smooth consistency.

2 Add a few drops of food coloring and mix well.

3 Frost the completely cooled cookies.

TIP: If you like, add sprinkles to the cookies before the icing hardens.

Seaweed Servers
What You Will Need

green or black heavy paper, cardboard, pencil, scissors, glue

1 Draw a seaweed shape onto the paper (see illustration) and cut out.

2 Glue onto cardboard and cut out.

3 Arrange the cookies on the server for your friends or family.

Starfish

Starfish—or sea stars—are some of the most colorful creatures found on the ocean floor. There are around 1,500 species of starfish that live in both warm tropical waters and cold polar regions.

Most starfish have five arms, also called rays, and a central body. But some species can have up to fifty rays. The purple sunstar often has between seven and thirteen rays. Some starfish have the special ability to regenerate (grow back) rays and other parts of their body if they are injured. The regrowth can take several months or even years.

dulse
(palmaria palmata)

common
starfish

purple
sunstar

common
sunstar

goose foot
starfish

Sparkly Seahorse Decoration

What You Will Need

tracing paper, pencil, tape, felt, two straight pins, scissors, 4-inch (10 cm) lengths of ribbon or yarn, glue, buttons, sequins

1 Trace the seahorse template twice (see instructions on page 3).

2 Pin both pieces of tracing paper onto the felt and cut around each shape. Unpin the paper.

3 Place the end of the ribbon or yarn on one seahorse head. Dot the whole seahorse with glue and place the second seahorse on top. Press them together to secure.

4 Glue buttons for eyes on both sides. Decorate both sides with sequins or small pieces of felt.

5 Leave your seahorse to dry and then hang it up!

SEAHORSE TEMPLATE

TIP: You can make both sides the same color or make them different.

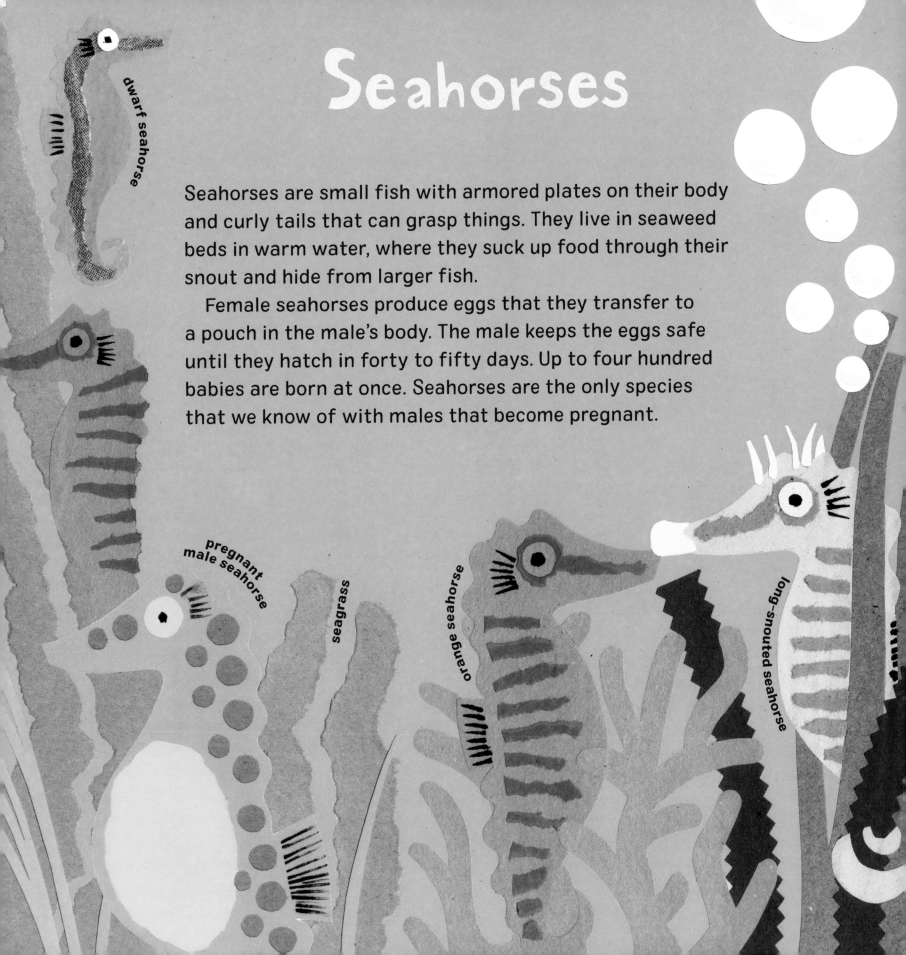

Seahorses

Seahorses are small fish with armored plates on their body and curly tails that can grasp things. They live in seaweed beds in warm water, where they suck up food through their snout and hide from larger fish.

Female seahorses produce eggs that they transfer to a pouch in the male's body. The male keeps the eggs safe until they hatch in forty to fifty days. Up to four hundred babies are born at once. Seahorses are the only species that we know of with males that become pregnant.

dwarf seahorse

pregnant male seahorse

seagrass

orange seahorse

long-snouted seahorse

Amazing Sea Creatures

What You Will Need

thick white paper, brightly colored crayons, black poster paint
and a large paintbrush, toothpicks

1 Color your white paper with colorful sections using crayons. Be sure
you make a thick layer of crayon and don't leave any white showing
when you're done. (See image 1 below.)

2 Paint over the colors with a layer of black paint and leave until it's
completely dry. (See image 2.)

3 Using a toothpick, lightly scratch through the paint to draw deep-sea
creatures. (See image 3.) Make them as amazing as you can! (See the
illustrations for inspiration.)

1

2

3

Boat Hat

What You Will Need

11 x 17 paper (tabloid size), scrap paper, toothpick, tape, markers

1 Fold the paper in half the short way with the fold at the top. Fold the top corners down to meet in the center. Fold up the bottom strip. Turn over and fold that bottom strip up, too. (See figure 1.) Smooth until flat.

2 Make a small flag with scrap paper and a toothpick, and tape it to the top of your hat.

3 Write your name or a number on the boat. Wear it proudly!

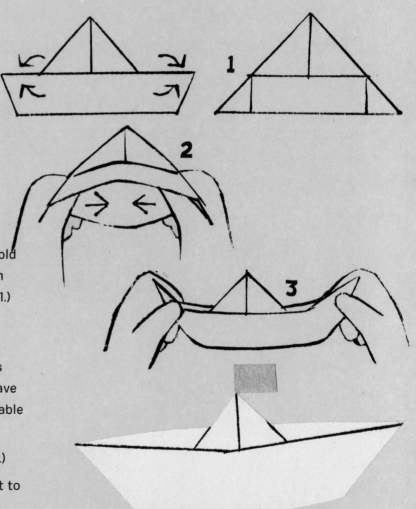

Paper Boat

What You Will Need

8½ x 11 paper (letter size), scrap paper, tape, toothpick, markers

1 Fold the paper in half the short way with the fold at the top. Fold the top corners down to meet in the center. Fold up the bottom strip. Turn over and fold that bottom strip up, too. (See figure 1.) Smooth until flat.

2 Place your thumbs inside the bottom of the boat and turn the strips upward (like turning them inside out). (See figure 2.) This can be tricky, but go slowly, and it'll work! The boat will now have a double thickness of paper around the bottom. Place on the table and smooth it out.

3 Pull the sides slightly apart to stand the boat up. (See figure 3.)

4 Make a small flag with scrap paper and a toothpick, and tape it to the top of your boat.

5 Write a name or number or decorate your boat.

TIP: You can use the boat like a bowl for snacks or try sailing it on water in the sink.

Nautical Flags

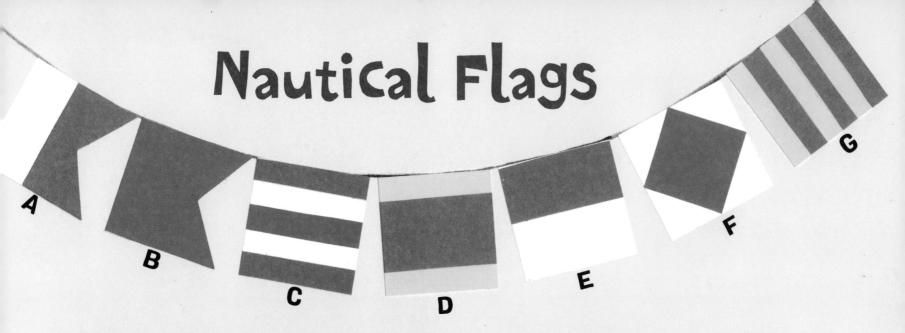

Nautical flags allow ships and boats to communicate with one another. They are also used to communicate with people on shore. There are twenty-six nautical flags that each stand for a different letter of the alphabet. Nautical flags use colors that can be easily seen and recognized at sea: red, blue, yellow, black, and white.

Ships can use the flags to spell out a message or use a single flag that stands for an entire message. For example, the flag for the letter A—alpha—tells other ships to keep clear because there is a diver underwater. Use "international maritime signal flags" to search online and learn the name and meaning for each flag.

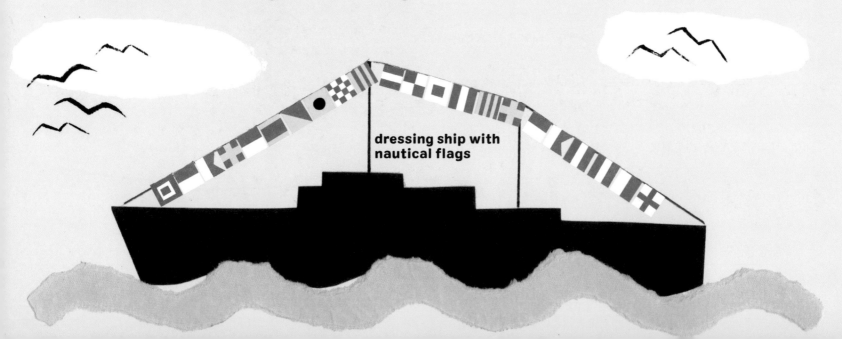

dressing ship with nautical flags

The International Code of Signals

Write a message or greeting, or write your name using nautical flags. (What do the messages on the boat on the opposite page and on the cake on this page say?)

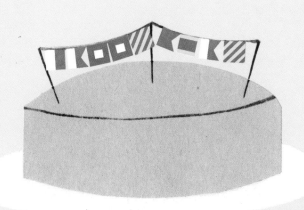

What You Will Need

white paper; pencil; ruler; scissors; yellow, blue, red, and black paint and paintbrushes (or markers/crayons in those colors); string or toothpicks; tape

1 Decide what your message will be and what you will use it for (perhaps as a banner or to decorate a cake). The purpose will determine the size of each square.

2 Cut the white paper into squares. Make as many as you need for your message in an appropriate size.

3 Paint or color them the right colors and patterns for each letter you need.

4 Tape the flags onto string to hang or onto toothpicks to decorate a cake.

octopus

shrimp

Published by Charlesbridge
85 Main Street
Watertown, MA 02472
(617) 926-0329
www.charlesbridge.com

First published in the UK in 2019 as *Ocean Book: Read,
Make and Create* by b small publishing ltd., 17 Aquarius, Eel
Pie Island, Twickenham, TW1 3EA | Text and illustrations copyright
© b small publishing 2019 | www.bsmall.co.uk

Printed in China
(hc) 10 9 8 7 6 5 4 3 2 1

Library of Congress Cataloging-in-Publication Data
Names: Beaton, Clare, author. | Haig, Rudi, author.
Title: Read, learn & create. The ocean craft book / written by
Clare Beaton & Rudi Haig ; illustrated by Clare Beaton.
Other titles: Ocean craft book | Read, learn and create.
Description: Watertown, MA : Charlesbridge, 2019.
"First published in the UK in 2019 by b small publishing, ltd."
Identifiers: LCCN 2018021350 (print) | LCCN 2018038360 (ebook) | ISBN
9781632896872 (ebook) | ISBN 9781632896889 (ebook pdf) | ISBN
9781580899413 (reinforced for library use)
Subjects: LCSH: Ocean--Juvenile literature. | Marine ecology--Juvenile
literature. | Nature study--Activity programs--Juvenile literature. |
Nature crafts--Juvenile literature.
Classification: LCC GC21.5 (ebook) | LCC GC21.5 .B43 2019 (print) | DDC
745.5083--dc23
LC record available at https://lccn.loc.gov/2018021350

Display type set in Potato Cut by Andrew Smith
Text type set in Colby by Jason Vandenberg
Printed by 1010 Printing International Limited in
    Huizhou, Guangdong, China
Production supervision by Brian G. Walker
Designed by Sarah Richards Taylor & Joyce White

sea fan

common whelk

oyster